You Forgot About Dre

About Dr. Dre

Dr. Dre is often considered the most influential rapper/producer of his time. With his straight-out-of-Compton attitude, Dre created his own style of hip-hop; one that went beyond flashy colorful clothes and fickle imagery, and coined the term and the sound that has become commonly known as gangsta-rap. In the tradition of bands like Cypress Hill and Parliament, Dre crafted his own subculture of sound. His G-funk ethic has been carried on in acts such as Snoop Doggy Dogg, Warren G and Ice Cube. His work in the famous N.W.A. collaboration, starring fellow rappers Eazy E and Ice Cube, revolutionized the rap industry forever. Dr. Dre was born Andre Young in 1965. He was reared by his mother and grandmother in a Compton housing project. At an early age Young was subjected to the gang influences of his environment, forming

This Is The Story Of Dr. Dre...

a rough and tough exterior that would later manifest itself in his music. Young became interested in hip-hop in the early 1980s and recorded several demos of his own productions. He also played clubs and house parties, making a name for himself in South Central Los Angeles. This is where he later collaborated with Ice Cube writing and producing material for Eazy E and his Ruthless Records enterprise. Eventually this partnership lead to the super-funk gangsta trio, N.W.A. (Niggaz With Attitude). By the time they had released their second album, *Straight Outta Compton*, N.W.A., with Dre's innovations, became nefarious for their hard core sound and controversial content. (They received a warning from the Federal Bureau of Investigation upon the release of their single "Fuck tha Police."

After the release of the successful 1990 EP *100 Miles and Runnin'* and its follow-up, *Efil4zaggin* ("Niggaz 4 Life" spelled backward), Dre made efforts to leave N.W.A. (Ice Cube departed the year before). By this time, Dre and partner Suge Knight were working on their own project, Death Row Records. When the manager of N.W.A. refused to let Dre out of his contract, however, Knight allegedly threatened his life in order to win the commodity that Dre had become. On his own in 1992, Dre released his first solo album, *The Chronic*, and began an alliance with Snoop Doggy Dogg, who helped the album gain its multi-platinum status. Singles like "Nuthin' but a G-Thang" and "Let Me Ride," exploited Dre's edgy, bold G-funk sound and, in the next four years, the album's influence on the industry became overwhelmingly apparent. Among his Death Row productions are the 1993 Snoop debut *Doggystyle* which made Snoop a household name. The success of Warren G.'s "Regulate" and Ice Cube's "Natural Born Killaz" are also credited to Dr. Dre. In a protest against long-time friend and partner Suge Knight, Dre left Death Row Records in 1996 and formed another label, Aftermath Records. His first effort, *Dr. Dre Presents...The Aftermath*, was released in 1996 and featured several other rap artists. "Been There Done That" became a hit single. Dre's *Chronic 2001*, dropped in November 1999.

—MTV

Albums

Chronic 2001
　　　　　Aftermath/Interscope, 1999

Dr. Dre Presents…The Aftermath
　　　　　Aftermath/Interscope, 1996

Back N Tha Day
　　　　　Blue Dolphin, 1996

First Round Knock Out
　　　　　Triple X, 1996

The Aftermath
　　　　　Aftermath/Interscope, 1996

Concrete Roots
　　　　　Triple X, 1994

Chronic
　　　　　Death Row, 1993

EPs + Singles

Keep Their Heads Ringin'
　　　　　Priority, 1995

Dre Day
　　　　　Death Row, 1994

Let Me Ride
　　　　　Death Row, 1993

Soundtracks + Other Appearances

Bulworth Soundtrack
Interscope Records, 1998
Dr. Dooom
Hieroglyphics
Invisibl Skratch Piklz
The Coup
Possible Suspects

Stats

- At the 2000 MTV Awards Dr. Dre won for the "Best Rap Video" *You Forgot About Dre.*

- Dr Dre's album *Chronic 2001* went 5 times Platinum in the U.S.

- Dr Dre's CD *Chronic 2001* went gold in Switzerland and Denmark.

- Dr. Dre's album *Chronic 2001* went Platinum in New Zealand and Australia.

- Dr Dre's album *Chronic 2001* went gold in Holland.

- Dr Dre's album *Chronic 2001* went 4 times Platinum in Canada.

- Dr. Dre's *Chronic 2001* album has been on the Billboard Charts forever.

- Dr. Dre's biggest tour up until now has been *Up In Smoke* with Eminem, Xzibit, Snoop Dogg, Warren G and Ice Cube.

About Eminem

Detroit MC Marshall Mathers (a.k.a. Eminem) released his debut 12" as one half of the two man crew, Soul Intent, and soon after released his '96 debut album, *Infinite*, featuring members of his crew, The Dirty Dozen. After being featured in *The Source's* Unsigned Hype column in '98, Eminem further made his name by dropping verses on indie singles by artists like Shabaam Sahdeeq and OldWorlDisorder. By the time he released his *Just Don't Give a Fuck 12"* and *Slim Shady EP*, Eminem was an underground sensation. Eminem's solid reputation as a lyricist earned him the respect of the powerful Dr. Dre, who signed him to his Aftermath label. Eminem's debut on Aftermath, *The Slim Shady LP*, hit No. 2 on the Billboard album charts within weeks of its release thanks to the breakthrough success of the single "My Name Is." Eminem received two awards at the 42nd Annual Grammys: Best Rap Solo Performance for "My Name Is" and Best Rap Album for *The Slim Shady LP*. He also records as one of the newer members of the

...And Eminem

New Jersey-based Outsidaz crew. Eminem's latest, *The Marshall Mathers LP*, was released in May 2000. The same year, Eminem won big at the MTV Video Music Awards, winning the Video of the Year and Best Male Video categories for *The Real Slim Shady*.

—MTV

Albums

The Slim Shady LP
> *Aftermath/Interscope, 1999*

Infinite
> *Web Entertainment, 1996*

Eps + Singles

My Name Is
> *Aftermath/Interscope, 1999*

Stats

- Won "Best Video" & "Best Male Video" at the MTV Music Awards for *The Real Slim Shady* (9/8/2000).

- Eminem's *The Slim Shady Album* was the first Rap album ever to go Gold in Norway (8/31/2000).

- Eminem's *The Slim Shady Album* went Gold in Korea (8/24/2000).

- Eminem's *The Slim Shady Album* went Gold in France and Poland (8/11/2000).

- The *Slim Shady LP* has remained on the Billboard Charts.

- The *Slim Shady LP* has gone Triple Platinum in the US.

- *The Marshall Mathers Album* has been on the Billboard Charts forever.

- *The Marshall Mathers Album* was released 5/23/2000 and was certified 6 times Platinum on 8/18/2000.

- Eminem's biggest tour up until now has been *Up In Smoke* with Dr. Dre, Xzibit, Snoop Dogg, Warren G and Ice Cube.

You Forgot About Dre!

The Unauthorized Biography of
Dr. Dre and Eminem
From N.W.A. To Slim Shady

A Tale of
Gangsta Rap, Violence, and Hit Records

By Kelly Kenyatta

Busta Books
Los Angeles

You Forgot About Dre!
The Unauthorized Biography of Dr. Dre and Eminem
A Tale of Gangsta Rap, Violence, and Hit Records
By Kelly Kenyatta

Published by: BUSTA Books
A Division of Amber Books
1334 East Chandler Boulevard, Suite 5-D67 Phoenix, AZ 85048
e-mail: bustabks@aol.com

ALL RIGHTS RESERVED

The publication is designed to provide accurate and authoritative information in regard to the subject matter covered. It is sold with the understanding that the publisher is not engaged in rendering legal, accounting, or other professional services. If legal advice or other expert assistance is required, the services of a competent professional person should be sought.

Amber Books are available at special discounts for bulk purchases, sales promotions, fundraising or educational purposes. For details, contact: Special Sales Department, Amber Books, 1334 East Chandler Boulevard, Suite 5-D67, Phoenix, AZ 86048, USA.

Library of Congress Cataloging-in Publication

Kenyatta, Kelly
    You forgot about Dre! : The unauthorized biography of Dr. Dre and Eminem : from
 NWA to Slim Shady, a tale of gangsta rap, violence, and hit records / by Kelly Kenyatta.
        p.cm.
  Includes bibliographical references.
  ISBN 0-9702224-9-1
    1. Doctor Dre. 2. Eminem (Musician) 3. Rap musicians--United States--Biography. I.
Title.

    ML394 , K48 2000
    782,421649'090'2--dc21
    [B]   00-051151

10 9 8 7 6 5 4

First Printing January 2001

Dedication

To Byron Kelly, Duke's illest Blue Devil
and
Christie Kelly (a.k.a. Diva Style)
running thangs in the South burbs

You are two awesome young people with
an abundance of gifts. Your stars will
shine brightly and ya know it.

Lotsa love,
Auntie

Contents

Introduction

When "gangsta rap" banged onto the music scene in the mid 1980's, it fascinated and intrigued young, urban African-Americans who rapped boastfully about running thangs in the ghetto—drinking, drugs, cars, money, smokin' muthafuckas, sex, bitches and ho's and an unfair justice system. Lyrics working together with a backdrop of undeniably soulful rhythms, gangsta rap was the bittersweet sound of the grimy, gritty inner city laid out in a fashion that was chic and seductive. Importantly, it was the music of a disenfranchised populace becoming further disenfranchised as crack cocaine entrenched itself into the community and into the psyche of the people. Nelson George, author of *Hip hop America*, is neither a legislator nor a politician, but he so insightfully points out what most American tax-supported public servants for years failed to realize in their scathing indictment of gangsta rap: that the music and crack rocks exploded in the urban areas at roughly the same time. "This is not a chicken-or-egg riddle," George notes, "first came crack rocks, then gangsta rap." Aside from drugs, gangsta rap is intertwined with broken families, failing school systems, faltering urban economies, racial and sexual discrimination, and a legal system that aggressively prosecutes and sentences crack cocaine users for low-level drug offenses.

In 1990, a Washington, D.C.-based nonprofit organization issued the startling report, *Young Black Men and the Criminal Justice System: A Growing National Problem*. The report showed a massive increase in the rate of young black males incarcerated or on probation—a quarter of the men between the ages of 20- and 29-years-old. That equaled 610,000 men, compared to 436,000 enrolled in college or vocational school.

It follows that these young adults would ferociously seek avenues of expression and empowerment. African-Americans have historically turned to music as a source of strength. Invariably, gangsta rap would be embraced by a great number of inner city young, black males. But urban America is not where gangsta rap ended, merely where it began.

Like an urgent mating call, the gangsta rap sound began piercing kids' ears across the country, from poor Latino city kids whose anguish was similar to that of poor black kids, to poor white kids, to upper-income black, Latino, Asian and white kids rebelling against their parents and adult domination. Whatever their beef, the irreverent in-your-face music stirred kids across the spectrum to crank up their sound systems and sing along, to feel empowered.

You Forgot About Dre! The Unauthorized Biography of Dr. Dre and Eminem is the coming of age story of two young men who by physical appearances are opposites. Yet, they bear stark similarities otherwise. Born to poor, teenage mothers, neither Dre nor Em was a member of America's privileged class. Both grew up in urban areas and were exposed to violence at an early age. Both developed a love for hip-hop so great that it exceeded all else. Having a disdain for rules and a passion for music, they both dropped out of high school to pursue rap. They have incredible focus, drive and work ethic. And their talent and zeal would propel them to achievements never before made in music.

This book chronicles Dr. Dre's boyhood days in Compton and his time with N.W.A. It is an account of how he, as a very young adult, dealt with the glitzy world of show business and the overwhelming pressures of fame—the women, the drinking, the wilding. It reveals how he and Marion "Suge" Knight formed one of the most powerful record labels in African-American history. It examines his relationship with Knight and other important industry figures like

Eazy-E, Snoop Dogg and Tupac Shakur. Importantly, this book follows the emotional growth of the gangsta rapper and imparts his sensitivity.

It paints a sheer and utter portrait of Eminem, a kid born into poverty and hard luck but a person who is a survivor. It chronicles Em's life as a boy shuttling between Kansas City, Missouri, and Detroit, Michigan, switching elementary schools as though they were socks. It is the story of a child living in fear of playground bullies but also of a child who managed to carve out a modicum of happiness and formed friendships that last until today. It is an account of how a couple of kids from nowhere become a music icon.

The Unauthorized Biography of Dr. Dre and Eminem is about a mentor and a protégé coming together to further impact hip-hop music and show the world that music is neither black nor white, but rather, a language of empowerment, creativity, and sweat.

Part 1

Dr. Dre

You Forgot About Dre!

Chapter 1

Straight Outta Compton:
A Star is Born

Some children are born with the proverbial "silver spoon" in their mouths. On February 18, 1965, Andre Young—a.k.a. Dr. Dre—was born into only a working class family in southern California. But better than a silver spoon, he was born with the Midas touch. As a toddler, Dr. Dre had a turntable at his fingertips and it would earn him tremendous gold and platinum. His future in Compton was precarious, however, as he grew up in the socially- and economically-changing town. The chances of him going astray and getting involved in crime were much greater than those of the young boy realizing his potential in the music industry.

But music was omnipresent in his home environment and he has said it might have saved him. Dre's earliest recollection of a passion for music goes back as far as his memory. The shelves in the Young household were lined with hundreds of his mother Verna's records. Artists like James Brown, Aretha Franklin, Marvin Gaye, Smokey Robinson and Diana Ross and the Supremes ruled in the music world and they took a strong hold in the lives of people all over the country, especially in Dre's house. Throughout his childhood, from Gladys Knight and the Pips to the Jacksons to funk masters Bootsy Collins and George Clinton, you could hear it all blaring from the Young's record player.

"I think music was my mom's release from the pressures of working two jobs and all," Dr. Dre said in a *Los Angeles Times* interview.

"When she got home at night, the stereo came on before the lights."

By age 3 or 4, Dre was enchanted with the black vinyls spinning on the turntable. On weekends, adults made their way to his house for his mom's card parties. The place would be packed with grownups eating, drinking, telling jokes, laughing, slapping cards down and talking trash. Just a toddler, Dre found it all very exciting.

"I would play the records," he recalled, adding that he loved stirring people up. "I'd put a record on and people would scream out and get up and dance."

Music and sports occupied a lot of Dre's time and kept him away from bad influences. In the 1960s, Compton was not a rough neighborhood, but rather a place of hope. Many African-American families who could leave the economically-depressed community of Watts did so en route to Compton. It was known as a nice community with fairer housing policies than some other towns. Compton was a palm-tree lined community that prospered. But things started to change during Dre's boyhood. Gangs were becoming prevalent in his area. Dre's parents separated when he was very young and he and his two siblings, Tyree and Shamika, were raised mostly by their mother. He looked out for the younger kids and they looked up to him. With their mother working, they formed an incredibly close bond. Dre's life was typical of a lot of young Compton kids who were happy because they were too young to understand the problems of adults.

"Compton was so much fun to me because it was so real," said Dre. "Where I lived was right next to Kelly park. I could jump the back fence and would be right there. There used to be a recreation center that is now a police sub-station. We used to throw dances there and later I started deejaying... When we weren't in the park, all the kids would be over at my house popping tapes into the deck. I was always playing around with the turntables, always practicing to perfect my skills."

Verna was a doting mother and a fiercely strong woman who protected her children from the harsh realities of their environment. While she struggled to make ends meet working two jobs, she required the kids only to go school, do their schoolwork and play. One Christmas she surprised Dre with his own turntable and that occupied him for years to come. He would spin records for his sister and brother and they would all fall asleep listening to music. But Verna wasn't certain just how long she could protect her children. She watched as her neighborhood changed rapidly before her eyes.

Once a predominately white community of middle-income families, whites fled Compton as more blacks moved in. Invariably, less attention was paid to the needs of the community in the areas of schools, recreational facilities, police protection and other tax-supported services. The town's income-level fell. All things considered, Compton was becoming increasingly vulnerable and attractive to street gangs and drug dealers. Dre's mother thought daily about the safety of her family. Somewhere during working hard and raising three children, she found a little time to date. She met a special man with whom she started spending quality time and eventually married. In some ways, things couldn't have been better for Dre who was by that time a teenager. His mom had found a significant other and with her new husband came three stepsisters and a stepbrother. As the families merged, Dre found not just a brother in his new sibling, but a future music collaborator. Dre's new stepbrother would make a name for himself as famous rapper Warren G.

Dre entered Centennial High School and did extremely well in some of his classes, well enough to earn a college scholarship to study mechanical drawing. But his real love was music. Every chance he got, he deejayed at parties. Davy-DMX was the first deejay he saw live, but he was most inspired by a record called "The Adventures of Grandmaster Flash on The Wheels of the Steel." He slipped into a popular club called The Eve After Dark to see other famous deejays whenever he could. Over the years, he would see hip-hop's best live and in person.

"Anybody who was anybody came to perform there, Kurtis Blow, LL Cool J, Public Enemy, Eric B. and Rakim...I saw them all," Dre said.

As a deejay, Dre first called himself "Dr. J" after one of his favorite basketball players, Los Angeles Laker Julius "Dr. J." Erving. Funk and R&B were big and Dre played it all, from George Clinton, Parliament and the Funkadelics to Bootsy Collins. He soon moved from deejaying at parties to deejaying in clubs. He got a job at The Eve After Dark and was having a blast. He found what he liked even more than funk was hip-hop, a bold and exciting new music where artists talked or "rapped" poetically to a soulful and rhythmic backdrop. This new sound came from the streets of New York block parties and park jams. Calling themselves deejays, a handful of music innovators performed this new music using catchy street names. Hip-hop was embraced largely by African-American and Latino post-soul-sick-of-disco kids hanging out, dancing and writing graffiti. It all started on the East Coast, but West Coast teens quickly took an interest in hip-hop.

Dre left school and joined the World Class Wreckin' Kru, one of the West Coast's earliest rap groups. He and his band mates tried to combine funk and hip-hop, which wasn't yet being done. Kru members went on stage in wild spandex jumpsuits accented with lace collars and sleeves. They topped off the costumes with capes. A humorous and clever Dr. Dre, who had adopted his current rap moniker, didn't surprise anybody when he decked himself out in a surgeon's gown and mask. The Wreckin Kru had some great times together although the group never made it big. Dre was a talented rapper and deejay, but he also was bright and enterprising beyond his years. He put out a single called "Dr. Dre's Surgery" on his own label and sold an estimated 50,000 copies. Although he did not put a dent in the national scene, he became a star in the Compton area. That taste of success would be his driving force to accomplish any goal he dared to envision.

Chapter 2

Attitude is everything: The forming of N.W.A.

Dre abandoned the idea of mixing funk and rap in favor of a new style he called "hardcore hip-hop," which the media would come to call "gangsta rap." Hardcore rappers didn't sugarcoat anything and worried little about whom they offended. Dre and his contemporaries rapped about ghetto life, the gritty, grimy, crime-infested streets of Compton, about run-ins with the police and gang shoot-outs, about poverty, dysfunctional relationships, ruthless women ("bitches" and "ho's") and whatever else was on their minds. The hip-hop scene was dominated by East Coast acts including the popular Public Enemy. Top East Coast rappers distinguished themselves with lyrics inspired by Malcolm X and African-American nationalist ideals. In California, a street-smart rapper named Eazy-E (Eric Wright) was looking into how he could carve out a bigger place on the map for West Coast rap. He used his business acumen—and money from his drug deals, he has said—to provide a venue for California artists to wreak havoc on the rap scene. Eazy-E started Ruthless Records, which provided an opportunity for some of rap's most influential performers to showcase their talent. Artists Ice-T, Schoolly D and Boogie Down Productions had already rapped about ghetto violence in their albums, but the Ruthless label group that followed them would leave an indelible print in the music industry. That group was N.W.A. (Niggaz With Attitude), co-founded in 1986 by Eazy-E, Dr. Dre and Ice Cube (O'Shea Jackson). Other members included DJ Yella (Antoine Carraby), the Arabian Prince and the D.O.C. A year later, MC Ren joined the group. N.W.A. would eventually produce lyrics about gangsta life in blunt and harsh language played to funky, melodic, bass-driven beats.

"People talk about how revolutionary N.W.A. was and how we had all these big ideas about how to change rap," Dre said in an interview with the *Los Angeles Times*. "But we were just making it for the neighborhood...We were making stuff we knew our friends would like."

N.W.A.'s first album, *N.W.A. and the Posse*, was a party jam record that didn't make much of a splash. But when the group revamped its style to become more violent, it hit big in 1988. The single "Fuck Tha Police" propelled the album Straight Outta Compton to colossal sales. Law enforcement officials and civic leaders were livid. The FBI paid N.W.A. a visit and accused members of glorifying violence to sell records. The bureau's disapproval of the rap group was made known to the public and debate heightened about the evils of gangsta rap. Coalitions formed and parents and religious, government and civic leaders decried the music. Most radio stations wouldn't play it. N.W.A. didn't seem to mind. Members noticed that the negative publicity they received seemed to have a positive correlation with record sales. Where music television shows and radio overlooked them, they grabbed headlines in major newspapers, were the subject of debate on CNN and got international attention because they were considered to be so outrageous.

Still, many people defended the music, asking "why shoot the messenger?" The kids were simply reporting street life in impoverished urban America, a place where American ideals had failed. While that might well have been true, N.W.A. members were still young and mostly just having a good time expressing themselves through music. Only later would they fully realize society's inequities. As a matter of fact, "Fuck Tha Police" was inspired by what began as a prank with Dre and some buddies.

He explained the impetus for the song to a *Times* reporter: "N.W.A. member Eazy-E and I were driving through Torrance, and Eazy was leaning out the window shooting people at bus stops with these paint guns that you can buy. We were laughing our asses off watching the people on the benches freak out because the paint balls were red. Well, not too much later we found ourselves down on the freeway with guns to our heads and the police were being like real assholes. We left that experience and went into the studio and made that song— the same day."

After the FBI attacked the song, which in fact seemed to help sales (*Straight Outta Compton* sold 600,000 copies in six weeks), N.W.A. looked for other things to say to "piss people off." The group put out *Efil4zaggin* (Niggaz 4 Life spelled backwards) in 1991 and it went straight to the top of the music charts, too. N.W.A. was a group of twenty-something men with a fist full of new money, fame and opportunities. Dre was a big handsome guy with a killer smile who attracted women in droves. He started partying harder than ever. He moved into a huge French colonial house that became the party headquarters.

Dre said in *The Guardian*, a London newspaper, "You could come over on Sunday morning and there's just people laying out on the floor asleep. Girls all over the place. I was spending money on a lot of cars, jewelry, apartments all over town. I probably bought somewhere between eight to 10 cars. Ferraris, I don't know how many Mercedes, Corvettes...It was dumb shit. I blew a lot of money. I was letting people in my life that were straight up there totally to see what they could get out of my pocket, and I wasn't seeing it. It was just another party to me, and you gotta have people around to have a party."

Dre was at the top of his game when the Youngs were unsuspectingly struck a blow that nearly paralyzed the family. Dre was on tour with N.W.A. when his girlfriend paged him on the road with the worst news an older brother could get. The girl sobbed into the telephone, "Dre, your brother, Tyree…Tyree. He's dead." After articulating the words, the girl yelled and cried uncontrollably and so did the family members and loved ones in the background. Dre's heart sunk. Although he had grown up and partied with Ice Cube, Eazy-E and a lot of the other fellas he was in the business with, his little brother was his best friend. "Why, Tyree. Why my baby brother?" "No, this can't be true." Dre's emotion ran amok. He couldn't believe it. He became angry, then sad. He went numb. It couldn't be. But it was true. Tyree had been attacked by a group of guys outside a store and they had broken his neck in the scuffle. Tyree had been killed and with him, he took a piece of his big brother.

"Dre cried," his mom, recalled with tears in her own eyes nearly ten years later. "It was the first time I had seen Andre cry since he was a little boy."

Dre found it very hard to accept that Tryee was no longer with him, his little brother whom he was so proud of, whom he had taught how to play ball, ride a bike and spin records, his little brother who had looked up to him, who had marveled when Dre brought home his first shiny new car. The death of his brother left a void in his soul but Dre and his family managed to keep going.

Everything was going well for Dre musically and monetarily, he was richer than ever before but he was becoming restless and began reacting to the pressures of being a high-rolling, rap superstar. Typical of young celebrities, he was finding himself overwhelmed with the negative aspects of fame—the constant attention, criticism, enemies, lack of privacy and the pressure to continuously outdo himself musically. One night in January 1991, the 26-year old just exploded. Dre had strolled into a music-industry party at a Hollywood club planning to have a good time with some of his friends but the evening erupted in a violent incident that would haunt him for years to come. Walking across the floor of the lavish, star-studded party, his eye caught 23-year-old Dee Barnes, the petite host of Fox TV's rap show "Pump It Up." Dre had been displeased with a segment Barnes had done that he felt painted himself and N.W.A. in a derogatory way so when he looked at her, he saw red. According to Barnes, Dre approached her and lifted her from the floor by her hair and ear. She managed to jerk away from the muscular, 6-foot-2-inch rapper and ran in terror into the ladies' room. She said Dre dashed after her, bursting through the crowd right into the ladies room where he grabbed her and threw her across the floor. Bystanders watched. Barnes recalled being too afraid of Dre to punch back. No one came to her rescue, she said, so she just stayed ducked down in a corner until Dre relented.

Before, Dre had only rapped about violence to women but the incident gave credence to rap critics' position that misogynistic lyrics were more formidable and deleterious than the industry would admit. Barnes filed a lawsuit of $22.7 million against Dre, who pleaded no contest to the beating. When the court's decision arrived, he was fined $2,500 and placed on probation for two years. He was ordered by the judge to perform 240 hours of community service and to produce an anti-violence public service announcement. A decision about the monetary award that Barnes sought was settled out of court. She was reported to have received a six-figure settlement.

The feeling of youthful invincibility would take a while to subside with Dre. Known by family and friends for his charm, goodness and loyalty, the testy Dre was emerging more frequently. Not long after the Dee Barnes incident, aspiring rap producer Damon Thomas charged that Dre broke his jaw during a brawl and Dre wound up in court again and was found guilty. He paid a $10,000 fine and was ordered to spend the next 90 days at home with an electronic monitoring device strapped around his ankle so that the police department would know his every move. Trouble continued. One evening Dre and a bunch of guests were having a barbecue at his house. The coals were dumped into a container that was pushed against the house. The house caught fire and while everyone escaped danger, Dre watched his grand home go up in flames.

An incident that grabbed the nation's attention was Dre's brawl with New Orleans' police. It was May of 1992 and he and an entourage were in the city for a convention of African-American radio executives. The hot movie "Mo Money" was premiering and Dre, other N.W.A. members and some friends wanted to see it. They went to the theater where it was playing, but were denied admittance. They walked a few blocks over to the News Orleans Sheraton Hotel where they were denied entrance to the lobby there, too. Police claimed the group needed passes to enter the hotel lobby where about 300 people were gathered. Dre and his friends were fuming at the back-to-back rejection and weren't willing to be turned away. Some of them made their way into the lobby anyway. When police attempted to kick them out, an alter- cation occurred. An estimated 50 people got caught up in the fiasco that resulted in two men getting cut before 80 officers could break it up. Dre was booked for battery on a police officer, inciting a riot, criminal damage and resisting arrest, according to a *United Press International* account of the incident. Dre was soon freed on bond and returned home.

Almost a decade later, he admits he was on a destructive path. He told *The Guardian*, "I was out of control. I was wildin' out, party- ing…I think the business, and all the fame and fortune sucked me in and I had to step back and see that I was ruining everything I had worked so hard at building."

He had built a brother-like relationship with Eazy-E over the years but that also was on the verge of collapse, according to insiders. Egos were clashing at Ruthless Records and things were getting uncomfortable. Dre would soon leave. But despite everything, he continued to build success in the industry.

You Forgot About Dre!

Chapter 3

Death Row

In 1992, Dr. Dre co-founded Death Row Records with former UNLV football star, Marion "Suge" Knight. Suge handled a lot of the business dealings of Death Row while Dre focused on the music. The highly ambitious entrepreneurs had entered into what appeared to be an ideal arrangement. They dreamed of Death Row becoming the Motown of rap music. Death Row managed to recruit artists whose music and names would become some of the most respected names in rap, including both Snoop Doggy Dogg and Tupac Shakur. Dre was at the height of his creativity. His album, *The Chronic*, in 1992, was the first released under the new record label, selling millions of copies while being praised as a masterpiece. With a swampy bass sythesizer, it incorporated the funk element and it was undeniably rich in R&B soul. The rapper and guest stars glorified gangster life in their sing-along choruses and laid-back, catchy rhymes. From its hot tracks "Nuthin' But A G' Thang," featuring Snoop, to "Let Me Ride" to "Rat-Tat-Tat," *The Chronic* was executed so well it made ghetto life seductive and chic.

The *New York Times* would later call it "the album that defined West Coast hip-hop." The paper wrote, "It's a hermetic sound, sealed off from street noise as if behind the windows of a limousine or a jacked-up jeep; it's the sound of the player enjoying ill-gotten gains but always watching his back. With its mixture of clarity and deep bass punch, Dr. Dre's tracks jump out of ordinary car radios as well as boom-boxes and fancy sound systems."

The Chronic was so appealing that mainstream radio opened up its airwaves to Dre's grooves. *Spin* magazine would name the Grammy-winning recording one of the 10 most important albums of the 1990s and the mega successful single "Nuthin' but a G' Thang" the best single of the decade. Retail sales for the album skyrocketed but the Chronic Tour scheduled to kick off early in the summer was postponed for several months. The rappers were suffering from too many legal woes. For one, Dre was still faced with old business. He was placed on house arrest for three months when he pleaded guilty to breaking a producer's jaws. Also during the summer, Snoop, who was emerging as an important member of the upcoming tour, was faced with serious trouble. Before the tour, Dre and Snoop were spending a lot of time together, first working on *The Chronic*, then on Snoop's debut album. Barely legal, 21-year-old Snoop was poised for stardom after rapping next to Dre on "Nuthin' But a G' Thang." He had also gained recognition for writing and performing the music for the film "Deep Cover," a track that appeared on *The Chronic*. Like Dre, Snoop's face had appeared in major publications, including *Source, Vibe* and *Rolling Stone*. Snoop's Dre-produced *Doggystyle* was expected to be released later that fall. The buzz was that it was going to be a hit from the moment it landed in record stores.

But late in the summer Snoop Dogg found himself in the wrong place at the wrong time and became embroiled in a murder scandal. He was said to have been driving his Jeep when his bodyguard, a passenger, allegedly shot a man who had been threatening them. The story according to Snoop's attorney, David Kenner, went like this: Phillip Waldermarian, 24, showed up outside Snoop's apartment in Culver City, California, and an argument broke out between him, Snoop's bodyguard McKinley Lee and associate Sean Abrams. Waldermarian was waving a gun, asking about Snoop's whereabouts and vowing to kill the rapper.

Snoop went downstairs but Waldermarian drove away.

Snoop, Lee and Abrams were driving around later and ran into Waldermarian in a park. Waldermarian went over to Snoop's vehicle and pulled a gun from his waistband looking as if he were going to fire. Lee shot him in self-defense, Kenner said, which is what a bodyguard is hired to do. Kenner told newspapers that Waldermarian, who was already on probation for publicly wielding a gun, had threatened Snoop a number of times in recent months. Kenner claimed that Waldermarian once held a gun to Snoop's head. He told the *Washington Post*, "There was a life-threatening situation, and (Lee) reacted to it." Other than driving the car to the studio, Snoop was uninvolved, he said.

The deputy district attorney for L.A.'s hard-core gang division, offered a different scenario that implicated Snoop as an instigator, though he did not accuse him of firing a gun.

Snoop had been scheduled to be a guest presenter on the MTV Music Video Awards show, so he kept his engagement then turned himself in on September 6. He was charged with a murder count that could have landed him in prison for life. His bail was set at $1 million. Lee was held without bail and Abrams' bond was set at $200,000. Death Row Records posted Snoop's bail and he was released the next morning. The following day the Chronic Tour kicked off with Dre and Snoop in Rochester, New York, but the whole tour foundered after a few performances.

If the legal woes of the rappers did indeed impede the Chronic Tour, the album, itself, continued to do well. *The Chronic* would reach an estimated $50 million in retail sales and *Doggystyle*, released in 1994 would reach $63 million. Tupac Shakur's All Eyez on Me," on which Dre was a producer, reached more than $65 million in sales. Just four years after Suge and Dre founded Death Row, it was estimated to be valued at $200 million. Death Row had become one of the most successful black-owned record labels in the history of music.

Dre once said, "I don't look for trouble but it seems like trouble just finds me." It did appear the two went hand-in-hand for a while. More problems were on the horizon. Death Row was experiencing success beyond belief, but there was a restlessness at the Los Angeles offices of the record label. Suge, a 6-foot-3-inch, 300-pound former body guard, supposedly went about business dealings with a vigilante style, following up with intimidation and in some cases, violence. There is talk that Suge once held Eazy-E at gunpoint and forced him to sign over Ruthless's rights to Dre's work. Whether that story is true, we might never know. But Suge did face assault charges for allegedly pistol-whipping two men in Death Row offices when he caught them using the office phone. Insiders said he showed no remorse and maintained the men deserved their punishment because he was waiting for a telephone call. Things got worse. Some employees feared going to work because gang members who were friends of Suge hung out at the offices to intimidate them. Even Dre was becoming increasingly dissatisfied with Death Row, although members were at first like a close-knit family watching out for each other and supporting one another. Many of the rappers looked up to Suge Knight in the beginning because if he believed in them, he would go to bat for them. And it wasn't just the rappers who saw his good points. Some of the residents of Compton talk about Suge's goodwill, like the Mother's Day dinners he threw. Suge was known to have given out turkeys to the needy on Thanksgiving and he played Santa to the neighborhood poor kids at Christmas. But the good times didn't last.

"It became, 'What kinda car does this person have. I gotta get a better car than that.' My house has to look better than that person's house,'" Dre said. "When the money started coming into play from Death Row, that's when the problems just went haywire."

"In the beginning, it was all about niggers coming up," Dre told *Blaze*. "Then it turned into a fucking Don Corleone thing. It was like a movie. You come into his (Suge's) office and can't step on the carpet's Death Row emblem and all that crazy shit. It didn't need to escalate like that...I got tired of seeing engineers get their ass beat for rewinding a tape too far."

It was then that he started thinking seriously about parting ways with Death Row.

Chapter 4

The Cell

Misfortune kept touching down all around Dre, some he looked for, some he didn't. One evening in 1994, he was drinking and decided he wanted to see how fast his Ferrari would go. He gunned the sports car to 140 miles per hour down Wilshire Boulevard in L.A., realizing shortly afterward he had engaged L.A.P.D. in a high speed chase. He stopped the car and was arrested on a drunk driving charge. He was found guilty of violating probation in the incident where he broke producer Damon Thomas's jaw. Dre would go to jail for the offense but would later see jail as his salvation during that time.

When Dr. Dre was sentenced to a Pasadena city jail for 180 days, his mom said it was "a blessing in disguise." Dre, no doubt, could have predicted his mom's response. After all, living smack in the middle of Compton, the Young family was no stranger to adversity. In fact, adversity had become a source of strength. Dre had seen what should have been misfortune turn itself into fortune many times, like when the FBI attacked N.W.A.'s music. The whole situation was turned around and their fans loved the group even more. Dre thought about what his mom said and in the end he agreed; there was a silver lining somewhere in the gray cell.

"To be honest, prison was probably the best thing that could have happened to me in my life," Dre told *The Guardian*. "Everything was happening so fast, the success I was having, all the money coming in, all the girls, all the partying. I never had a chance to say, 'Yo, what do I want life to hold?' I had to find myself. And it was crazy. I saw a confused individual. A guy that wasn't sure what he really wanted out of life. It mad me say, 'Yo, man, fuck those streets, fuck everything that's going on out there on those streets. Is this the life I wanna lead, or do I wanna be a business-man, be able to take care of my family, chill out, have fun and make money while I'm sleeping?'"

Day after day, long night after long night, Dre sat in jail with nothing to do but think about how he was destroying his life. Feel-ing forsaken in the cold, small cell, he thought of his late brother often. Miracu-lously, Tyree came to his rescue in his dark-est times. An angel to watch over Dre, Tryee would not leave his side. Dre's life took a turn for the better the way his mother had told him it would.

It was while he was jailed that he received the news that Eazy-E, who was a notorious womanizer, was dying of AIDS. Dre rushed to the hospital but Eazy had just fallen into a coma. He died nine days later. Dre was distraught. The wrangling he and Eazy had had over the past few years had not erased the love and friendship they'd developed as young boys. Eazy had been like a brother to him and even today, Dre is sorry they hadn't gotten around to reconciling their differences. When he walked away from the Pasadena jail, he had given serious thought to what was and what was not important in life. He set out to reclaim his peace of mind and that would include severing all ties with Death Row.

▲▲▲

In 1996, Snoop Dogg went on trial for murder and was found not guilty. While Snoop's acquittal was good news to Death Row, bad news devastated the hip-hop nation. Up and coming prodigy Tupac Shakur was shot dead while sitting in a car next to Suge Knight. Dre and Tupac had become friends and the news of Tupac's death deeply saddened him. It also was another eye opener him. He was lucky that he hadn't been in the car, too. Suge was shot in the incident but he surived. He did not escape jail. He was reportedly caught on camera taking part in the beating of a gang member who was an enemy of his associates. He had had a string of run-ins with the law and eventually violated the terms of his probation for assaulting the two other men with a pistol. The record industry mogul was sentenced to nine years in prison and the curtain fell on Death Row.

Today, Dre considers Death Row a closed chapter in his life. But he said he left because it stopped being fun. It wasn't easy to leave, he said. It was difficult, like a divorce.

Chapter 5

In the Aftermath

Dr. Dre gave up the wild single life and married Nicole, a talented and attractive interior decorator he had been dating for some time. He later moved with his wife and their two children to a gorgeous, three-story home on an enormous estate in San Fernando Valley, Calif. He admits he likes the high life and would continue selling records to insure that lifestyle.

"I don't even miss going out to parties and clubs," Dre said, after turning over a new leaf. "Whenever we want to have a function, we do our own thing, real private with just people that we know. We will turn the music up, have drinks and party, but it's a lot more comfortable."

Dre forged ahead on plans to develop his own new record company. Interscope was one of the companies interested in backing him. Interscope's co-owner Jimmy Iovine, who produced rock superstars U2 and Tom Petty, also was a big fan of Dre's work and wanted to invest in his new venture. With Interscope's backing, Dre formed Aftermath.

"Dre's work is stunning," Iovine said. "We fought very hard to close the deal with him because we believe he is a brilliant innovator."

Dre's first release was *Dr. Dre Presents the Aftermath* in 1997. The album was a compilation of singles by unknown artists. It was not as hardcore as what his fans were accustomed to. The album did well commercially, but it paled in comparison to the producer's past successes. Dre recalled after the release that he wasn't getting compliments from his fans. People were expecting 7-Up and they got water. Some critics said that the great producer had lost his edge. Dre turned to Nicole for consolation. She told him he needed to return to his hardcore roots. She helped him remember that his business was entertainment and that it was important to give his fans what they wanted. After getting married, Dre felt uncomfortable rapping about scoring with women and using street language like "bitches" and "ho's" even if he was describing groupies, gold diggers and manipulators. Was it possible that Dre was buying into what all the critics had said over the years, that his music in part caused society's ills? Would he compromise his art?

He would not. The doctor took the advice of his wife and by doing that, he followed his own heart, too. And he went with his fans who wanted to hear "Dre be Dre." When he dropped his next album *Dr. Dre 2001* in 1999, his fans knew he was back.

MTV wrote, "*Dr. Dre 2001* has only just hit record stores and judging from the early response to his first single, 'Still D.R.E.,' it looks as if Dr. Dre may have delivered the antidote to those suffering from 'Chronic'-haters disease."

In this album, Dre managed to strike a balance that reflected his personal growth while still giving fans ample servings of hardcore hip-hop—dope rhythms, bawdy sex , profanity and violence. His guest line up included Snoop Dogg, Hittman, Kurupt, Nate Dogg, Xzibit, Ms. Roq and other hot acts.

About his producing technique, he said: "Together with my bass player and myself on the drum-machine, we play around until something sparks me. When I'm sparked, that's when it's time to get creative and begin to orchestrate."

He strategically launched the album with a hot single "Still D.R.E.," which featured Snoop Dogg. "I thought that would be a good way to introduce myself back to the public, and it's just an energetic song. When it comes on in the clubs, people go crazy. Also, when we do it live, people go wild. It's an excellent first single," he said.

When Dre did the "Still D.R.E." video, it was received well by fans, too, possibly because he returned to vintage Dre, the gangsta thang.

He explained, "I chose to do the video to "Still D.R.E" that way because a lot of people out in the streets were like, 'Yo, when you going to get back to some of that "Nuthin But a G Thang," "Let Me Ride" kinda joint?' I was like, 'Okay, well, let me try to hit 'em with this and just make it still look a little futuristic.' So we had to take it back to the neighborhood, take it back to the cars, you know, the girls dancing, and everybody just having a real fun time."

"It felt real good to get back with all the guys from the first *Chronic* album. When they came in the studio, it was just like we were never apart," Dre told MTV. "It was a weird feeling, like, okay, everybody just came in and grabbed pens and papers and, you know, (started) doing they thang. It was just fun. Lot of laughter, and we had fun doing the songs."

Some people believed *2001* resonated with fans because Dre opened up and shared more of himself. For the first time, he expressed his deep feelings about the death of his younger brother. He remembered Tyree in "The Message," a ballad that featuring R&B superstar Mary J. Blige.

"Back in the day, I would never have made a song about my brother, but it was a very big part of my life," Dre said, "I finally decided to give people that much more of me."

On "Real Gangstas Don't Cry," Dre shows his "only human" side when he says, "if that's the truth then I'm realizing I ain't no gangsta."

"People definitely had the wrong idea about me," he said. "A lot of people were saying I was a mean cat, I disrespected women, a lotta bullshit, a lotta nonsense. Of course I can't blame them, but I'm a different person today. I can't blame them, and that's why I wanted to do this album and present myself in a new light—the Dre of today."

Another 2001 artist that rap lovers were eager to hear was Dre's latest protégé, Eminem, who was featured on the popular "Forgot About Dre" track. Dre had discovered the talented rapper in 1997. He later produced Eminem's single "My Name Is" and it had been a smashing success, a prelude to the unimaginable musical achievements that would soon follow. Eminem was a white rapper with a rough street upbringing who—with capability and authenticity—would quickly gain the respect of established artists like Missy Elliott, Snoop, Mary J. Blige and Ice-T. Similar to N.W.A., Eminem almost instantly gained a huge following of well-to-do suburban kids with ripe rebellion.

Dre scored big when he signed Eminem to Aftermath and worked with him on his records. Eminem would emerge as a best-selling, record-breaking superstar who was no less controversial than Dre himself. Dre, together with Eminem, would further broaden the scope of the hip-hop genre. Arguably, hip-hop had long had a sizable white following and there had been a number of popular white rappers. Vanilla Ice was hot in 1990 with "Ice Ice Baby," but fell from grace after being accused of stealing another artist's work and forging his background to appear more "street." The Beastie Boys broke rap album sales records in the late 80's with "Licensed to Ill." But there were no major white rap artists as of late. Dre and Eminem, the "Dreem Team," would unite rap fans across color lines and remind the world that everything—especially music—isn't so black or white. Many a doubter wondered if Eminem had what it takes to gain acceptance in the hard-to-earn-respect world of hardcore hip-hop. Dre wasn't concerned for one minute about that.

"I wasn't worried that people would react against him because he's white. The hardest thugs I know think this white boy's tight," he said.

Dre on stage, Up in Smoke Tour

Photo by Raymond Boyd

Em, Up in Smoke Tour

Photo by Walik Gorshorn

Dre, Up in Smoke Tour

Photo by Walik Goshorn

Em's 2000 Marshall Mather's Album Release at Club One51 in NYC. (l to r) Missy Elliot, Eminem, Aaliyah, and Timbaland

Em's 2000 Album Release Party, Club One51 with Eve
Photo by Walik Gorshorn

Snoop Dogg and Dr. Dre

Photo by Raymond Boyd

Eminem at 2000 Album Release in New York, Club One51
Photo by Walik Goshorn

Up in Smoke Tour, Nassua Coliseum

Photo by Walik Goshorn

(l to r) Kurupt, Nate Dogg and Warren G. backstage at the Up in Smoke Tour, Continental Airlines Arena, NJ

photo by Walik Goshorn

Dre, Rap's Greatest Record Producer

Photo by Raymond Boyd

Snoop and Eve backstage at Hot 97s Summer Jam Concert at the Continental Airlines Arena.

Photo by Walik Goshorn

Ice Cube backstage at Up in Smoke Tour Venue, Continental Airlines Arena, East Rutherford, NJ
Photo by Walik Goshorn

Snoop Dogg backstage, Up in Smoke Tour

Photo by Raymond Boyd

Eminem 2000 Album Release Party, Club One51, NY
Photo by Walik Goshorn

(l to r) Damon Dash, Snoop,UGK, and DJ Clue
Photo by Walik Goshorn

Snoop Dogg at the "Dogfather's" release party.

Dr. Dre and his wife, Nicole pose for a photo at Dre's "Aftermath" party in Chicago.

Photo by Raymond Boyd

*Dre and sons backstage, Up in Smoke Tour, Continental Airlines
Arena, East Rutherford, NJ*

Photo by Walik Goshorn

Sporting a rare smile, Snoop Dogg meets a fan at George's Music Room in Chicago.

Photo by Raymond Boyd

Hot 97's Summer Jam
Eminem at the Continental Airlines Arena, East Rutherford, NJ
Photo Walik Goshorn

Eminem

Photo by Walik Gorshon

Dr. Dre, World's Greatest

Photo by Walik Goshorn

Nate Dogg, Snoop Dogg, Kurupt (behind Snoop),Dre: Free Flowing

Photo by Walik Gorshon

Eminem, The Real Slim Shady

Photo by Walik Goshorn

Part 2

Eminem

You Forgot About Dre!

Chapter 6

The Coming of Age of
Marshall Bruce Mathers, III

His heart racing, a blue-eyed, fair-skinned boy lurked around in the neighborhood store anxiously awaiting an opportunity to grab a pack of cigarettes and shove them into his pocket before anyone noticed. After skulking out of the store, he took the cigarettes home to his mother. Just once more, Marshall Mathers, III, a.k.a, Eminem, would save himself from the embarrassment of appearing destitute in front of his school mates. While his mother had given him the money for the cigarettes, he wanted to use it for something else.

"I would steal the cigarettes, keep the $2 for lunch," Eminem explained to a reporter. "I was on free lunch at school. If a girl is standing behind you in line and you liked that girl and she sees that you're on free lunch, then the gig is up—know what I'm sayin'? And you feel shitty. So I used to take the money for cigarettes and act like I ain't on welfare."

Gone are the days when Eminem has to sweat finances. He has arrived as one of the most popular rap artists in the industry. He burst onto the music scene in 1999 with *The Slim Shady LP*. Eminem's style is bold. He says whatever he wants and that endears him to his fans—many millions of them who have sent sales right through the ceiling in a record-breaking fashion. Eminem's foes criticize him for his lyrics which they say are misogynistic and violent, and poisonous to the young minds of his fans. But like rappers before him, he makes no apologies. He was born to a 15-year-old mother on October 17, 1972, in St. Joseph, Missouri. He says he never knew his father. Eminem's life has been rough and in many instances he is simply rapping about what he has been through. In some other cases he's obviously joking, he says, and he takes issue with people who don't listen to his lyrics enough to know the difference.

Eminem said in the *Washington Post*, "I'm a guy and I have been through a lot of shit, a lot of fucked-up relationships, so what I'm doing is reflecting what I know. You've got to live it. You've got to see what I went through. I wish I would have had a video camera following me everywhere I went when I was growing up. You got to see what I lived in."

Although Eminem never knew his father, his anger flares up today when he talks about him. "I don't give a fuck if my mother was bad to him or if she cheated on him. Whatever the cause is, that ain't got shit to do with me. He could've reached out," he told *Vibe*.

▶▶▶

As a little boy, Em never settled into a neighborhood. His mother, Deborah Mathers-Briggs, moved with the toddler to a rough neighborhood in Detroit and they would move back and forth between Kansas City and Detroit until he was a teenager, supposedly at least 10 times before he was 10 years old. He attended five different elementary schools in four cities during that time. Oftentimes, Eminem and his mother ended up living with relatives and friends. And when they lived in their own places, the neighborhoods were never nice because he says his mother didn't hold down steady work. He vividly remembers the time he was kicked, beaten and left bruised and unconscious on the playground by the school bully when he was in third grade. It took a dozen doctors costing $500,000 to restore the young boy to health.

In one particular east Detroit community, Em was always on the run from the bullies at school or from street gang members. He became a great distance-runner as a way to survive. One time he almost did not survive, like the time he flipped the finger to a carload of kids who had flipped him off. The kids stopped the car and grabbed him before he could escape. At gunpoint they made him take off all of his clothes except his socks and underpants. Terror went through his body like lightening. What would they do next? Luckily for Eminem, he didn't have to find out. A truck driver stopped and pulled a gun on his attackers, pulled Eminem into the cab of the truck and drove away from the scene. And incidents like that would color his world in shades of gray and blue for years to come.

Eminem recalled in *The Guardian*, "I was always getting jumped on, dog! On the way to school, on the way back from school. I was always getting fucked with. Why? I was puny, timid. I didn't do weights until I was 17. And I lived in a fucked-up neighborhood where there was always some kind of drama."

Through it all, a few stars happened to shine in the rapper's dismal life. There was his Uncle Ronnie, a friend named Proof, who is now a support act in his shows, and Kim, who would become his wife. So between a mostly unhappy home-life and a hellish school experience, Eminem still managed to dream, first of being a comic book artist and later a rapper. It was his uncle and best friend Ronnie, who was almost his own age, who nurtured his interest in rap music. One day Ronnie gave him Ice-T's single "Reckless." He fell in love with the song and so his love for the rap genre began. Ronnie and he talked about rap music and created rhymes and the whole ominous cloud that hung over his childhood disappeared, if only for a day. Eminem spent endless hours studying the styles of LL Cool J, Run-DMC and the Beastie Boys. He read the dictionary to learn more words to improve his rhymes. He went to friends' houses a lot to rap, especially to Proof's house. At other times he stayed in his room, standing in front of the mirror rapping and assessing himself. After hearing tracks from the Beastie Boys' 1986 album *Licensed to Ill*, Eminem would try to emulate them.

"I didn't know they were white," he said. "I just thought it was the craziest shit I had ever heard...Then I saw the video and saw that they were white, and I went, 'Wow.' I thought, 'Hey, I can do this.'"

"My life wasn't always depressed and dark," he said in *The Guardian*, adding that he still occasionally misses certain things like "running in the streets and hanging out." "The good things were just being young and buying the hottest new albums and when I got kicked out of my house, I'd be 'fuck it,' and go round to Proof's."

He remembers how neither Proof nor he ever had much money, but their friendship made things more livable. Actually, it was Proof's friendship and rap music that made life more livable. When Eminem was 13, he went to his first rap concert and his love for hip-hop strengthened. His dream of being a rapper was reinforced. He kept practicing his rhymes and perfecting his skills through his freshman year in 1986 at Lincoln High School in Warren, a suburb of Detroit. Maybe Em practiced too much. When the end of the school year rolled around, he found he had flunked. His interest in school declined even further and he failed his second attempt at ninth-grade, too.

"That wasn't because I'm stupid or nothing. It was just because I never went to school," he told a *Washington Post* reporter. "I was enrolled, but I just never went. I always wanted to rap. Me and Proof used to skip school together because we always was, like, you know, all we wanted to do is rap. 'I ain't gotta work; I ain't gotta go to school; I ain't gotta finish my education. I'm gonna rap. I'm gonna be a rapper one day,' you know. And we had these little dreams."

After his third attempt at ninth-grade, Eminem dropped out of school. In the years that followed, he pursued rapping. When he wasn't hanging with Proof, he was with his uncle Ronnie who was perhaps his most avid fan. And then one day while he was at a friend's house, he met a pretty 13-year-old girl named Kimberly. Eminem was putting on a show for his friends, lip-synching to LL Cool J and Kim was obviously charmed by his act. Then 15, Eminem was smitten and started going out with her. He walked many a day through rough neighborhoods to get to Kim's section of town. Sometimes he would get beaten up on his way to visit her. Once he even got shot at but he would not be deterred. A very special bond was developing and both were determined that nothing would come between them. They would walk down the railroad tracks together, and there, no one bothered them. Eminem and Kim became like Bonnie and Clyde; they were best friends and stuck together over the years through many rough times.

▲▲▲

Eminem never lost sight of his music. He put his raps on cassettes and sold them in local record stores or wherever he could. He held odd jobs to take care of himself. He was working with record labels who strung him along, but he was hopeful to strike something solid. His relationship with Kim matured and years after they met, their daughter Hailie Jade was born one Christmas Day. Eminem found a job in 1996 at Gilbert's Lodge, a restaurant in St. Clair Shores, where he would stay for a couple of years. That was one of the most disciplined times of his life because the same year he started working at the restaurant, he put out *Infinite*, his first full-length album. He so desperately wanted to be accepted on Motor City's hip-hop scene that he rapped in a way he thought would be most accepted. He said that with *Infinite*, he was trying to figure out how he wanted his rap style to be, how he wanted to sound and present himself on microphone. He chalked that album up to being a part of his growing stage.

The album did not sell well and Eminem was disappointed and hurt by the response it received. But he became more determined and forged ahead on other music, which would become The *Slim Shady EP.* He abandoned the idea of trying to gain acceptance and wrote for himself. On that record he vented, he ranted and he raged. He spewed venom at the local music industry personalities. And he ranted about life in general. The set went over big with the picky hip-hop underground.

"I had nothing to lose, but something to gain," Eminem said on vh1.com. "If I made an album for me and it was to my satisfaction, then I succeeded. If I didn't, then my producers were going to give up on the whole rap thing we were doing. I made some shit that I wanted to hear. *The Slim Shady EP,* I lashed out on everybody who talked shit about me."

He meanwhile sent demos of his music to Paul Rosenberg, who would soon after become his manager. The two had some history together and Rosenberg knew the rapper's work. He was a suburbanite in law school when he first saw Eminem at one of the performances. He never aspired to rap, but he was a fan of hip-hop and he dreamed of working in the music business. Rosenberg was encouraged when he heard Eminem's edgier material. After he became the rapper's manager, he entered him in some rap competitions and presented the new tape to record executives.

Eminem also had given Wendy Day of the Rap Coalition a copy of the *Infinite* album. She helped him secure a spot at the Coalition's 1997 Rap Olympics in Los Angeles. He packed his bags and headed to California to compete in the Los Angeles Rap Olympics with the hope of winning and being discovered. He was being evicted, so he really needed the prize money and notoriety the contest could yield. He came in second place in the major open-mike contests. But second wasn't enough to earn him a contract. He returned to Detroit at an all-time low. He got fired from the restaurant. At one point, when he recorded the song "Rock Bottom," he even made what he calls a "dumb attempt" at suicide when he learned that a guy who was supposed to give him a record deal actually worked in the mailroom of the record label. Eminem recalls he took a bunch of pills and then puked all over the bathroom.

"I was really depressed," he said, maintaining he really wasn't trying to kill himself as much as trying to get attention. "It wasn't like a deliberate attempt. If I wanted to end my life, I would end my life."

It was a good thing for Em that he lived. True to the adage that the darkest hours are just before dawn, his life would take a turn for the better. He recorded the underground classic "5 Star Generals" and because of that, he gained some recognition in Japan, New York and Los Angeles. The recording helped him earn a spot on the Lyricist Lounge Tour and he traveled in concert from Philadelphia to Los Angeles.

But Eminem's biggest break of all came when his music landed upon Dr. Dre's ear. Eminem had left one of his CDs with Jimmy Iovine. Dre saw it laying on the floor of Iovine's garage and was attracted to the cover. He picked the tape up and listened to it and was very impressed. He called Eminem to talk. When some friends told Em that "some guy calling himself a doctor" had called about his music, he thought they were joking. But Dre had called him to tell him how much he liked his music. He wanted to sign him to his record label.

"It was an honor to hear the words out of Dre's mouth that he liked my shit," Eminem said on vh1.com. "Growing up, I was one of the biggest fans of N.W.A., from putting on the sunglasses and looking in the mirror and lip-synching to wanting to be Dr. Dre, to be Ice Cube. This is the biggest hip-hop producer ever."

Dre signed Eminem to Aftermath and after that, the hard-luck kid from the Midwest would experience fame beyond what he possibly ever dreamed.

Chapter 7

Slim Shady in the House

The *Slim Shady LP* was released in 1999 and its hot single "My Name Is" burned up the airwaves. MTV appeared to fall in love with Eminem at first sight. But from the moment he caught the attention of mainstream America, he was controversial. The artist had a lot going on that could be considered both good and bad. To his credit, he had serious rhyming abilities. He was the protégé of Dr. Dre, who is regarded as one of the best hip-hop producers around. Other important rappers, including Missy Elliott, talked Em up from jump street. There was the "Great White Hope" factor that the media pointed out: hip-hop's white fans were excited to see a talented white rapper arrive in an arena where they are a minority. To boot, Eminem had heart-throb looks and a bad-boy way about himself that made teenage girls swarm record stores. But Em's lyrics did not go over well with everybody. *Billboard* magazine had run an editorial by Editor in Chief Timothy White months before the release of the album accusing Eminem and the industry that supported him of exploiting the world's misery. Like other rappers before him who blew up the scene, Em was revered by his fans, yet reviled by large numbers of parents, journalists and other rap detractors. But the more people talked, whether good or bad, the more his music sold.

CMJ New Music Report wrote that Eminem had been "burning up the underground with his scorching debut single." Eminem paired "Redman's gutter humor and meta-phorical dexterity with Canibus' raging themes" to match the high expectations surrounding his brilliant new album, the review said. "Doing his mentor Dr. Dre proud, Eminem follows the N.W.A. heritage and leaves even the raunchiest MCs shocked as he weaves poignant tales of the abused outsider with the compelling twists of a Slick Rick track. From the rugged confession "Guilty Conscience" to the radio-friendly "My Name Is...," Eminem drops dope lyrics over DJ Muggs-inspired productions."

Rapper Ice-Tea told *Entertainment Weekly*, "What he's doing is shock rap, but because he's a white kid he's blowing everybody's minds. If you listen to his album, his black buddies rhyme just like him but it's not as good because you're used to black kids talking crazy. When you hear a white kid doing it, it sounds way crazier. Plus he's got a lot of skill, he knows what he's doing, he's paid his dues."

Within two weeks of its release, *The Slim Shady LP* raced to number 2 on the *Billboard* charts and would stay on *Billboard* Top 200 for 38 weeks. Nine months after its release, the LP had sold 2.6 million copies.

One critic described the track "My Name Is" as "a twisted and hilarious stream-of-consciousness romp over a rather large Dr. Dre-produced beat." On *The Slim Shady LP*, Eminem, through his alter ego (Slim Shady) raps about being "white trash, broke, and always poor." He raps about what he knows, like working on lousy jobs for dirt-low wages. He laments losing friends to drugs. On one track, he wonders if he'll have enough money to support his family. And he rails against his parents, which would result in a lawsuit by his mother. Some praised Eminem for his fast-paced lyrics, calling them humorous. Others thought his message was often sad. And still others saw his rap as provocative, violent and misogynistic. On the single "97 Bonnie and Clyde," the rapper pretends to murder his daughter's mother and heads off to the beach at night to get rid of the body.

Records are like movies, Eminem explains. The only difference is there's no screen with his music. One day he was sitting around with Dre talking about writing a song about someone contemplating an evil act. During the brainstorming session, a scene from the movie "Animal House" popped into his head. In that particular scene, a girl walks by a guy and the guy is thinking about raping her. A devil perches itself on one of the guys shoulder and an angel on the other. The angel says don't do it and the guy does not. Why is it, Em asked, that he is criticized for his single "Guilty Conscience" because of the rape fantasy when the idea came from the movie "Animal House," which was extremely popular? Dr. Dre had asked the same question a decade before but no one seemed to have an answer then, either.

▲▲▲

Em's life moved at whirlwind speed. He was reaching new heights when he experienced an all-time low. In 1999, Eminem's best friend and uncle Ronnie died and that sent the rapper into a state of shock. A newspaper account of the incident said Ronnie died in an accidental shooting but Em believed it was a suicide. He said his uncle shot himself after an argument with a girlfriend but Em couldn't understand it: "I've been depressed and had situations when I took too many of this or too much of that, but never really wanting to kill myself. I've got a daughter and I want to look after her. I think if Ronnie had someone in his life like I have a daughter, he would still be here today."

Eminem immersed himself further into his work. Ronnie had been his biggest fan. He would not fail his uncle now. *Rolling Stone* had picked Eminem as its cover boy less than two months after *The Slim Shady LP* album came out. When the magazine was published, the headline screamed "Low-Down and Dirty White-Boy Rap: Eminem's Twisted Life Story." Should Eminem have been insulted? Hardly. The story appealed to his fans and he didn't care much about his foes. Eminem went all out to promote his album giving about 100 interviews and putting on two shows a day during one period. He thought of little other than work. His daughter Hailie Jade would call sometimes and he wouldn't have time to talk to her, which was unlike him. During a rock tour, the Warped Tour, he was stretching himself very thin. He performed during the day for the mostly rock audience, then drove for hours to perform later the same night for a rap club. Then he would go back and join the Warped Tour.

By the time the tour neared the end, Eminem was on the verge of exhaustion. One night he hurried onto a stage to perform, not realizing the stage was drenched in beer and water. He slipped and tumbled about ten feet, landing on the club's floor and some busted ribs. It took that fall, he recalls, to slow him down and restore his schedule to some normalcy.

Meanwhile, Deborah Mathers-Briggs was one of those who did not particularly care for Eminem's act. The rapper would find himself, just days before Thanksgiving in 1999, squared off in a public arena to do battle with his mother. She was miffed at her son's comments about her being a drug user who collected welfare checks in various media interviews. She hired attorney Fred Gibson and filed a lawsuit against her son. Her lawsuit claimed statements he made damaged her reputation and also caused insomnia, anxiety and emotional distress. She sought a $10 million settlement. Em put a legal team on the case. If his mom's attempt to get his money did indeed dampen his spirit, he kept right on going.

As Grammy time rolled around for 2000, Em's name was dropping in the same conversations as some of hip-hop's most popular artists, like Busta Rhymes, Missy Elliott, Puff Daddy, Will Smith, The Roots, Q-Tip, and even Dr. Dre. A Los Angeles journalist noted that in the rap category, Eminem deserved to win for his "witty and warped" *The Slim Shady LP*. He did, scoring two awards: for Best Rap Album and Best Rap Solo Performance.

Chapter 8

The Marshall Mathers LP

Through the touring, publicity, attacks by foes and legal and relationship problems, Eminem found time within a year to record his next album on the After-math/Interscope label. Executive produced by Dr. Dre, the album featured a number of hot artists including Dre, RBX, Sticky Fingaz, Dido and Snoop Dogg. Fans were hungry for Eminem's new album and immediately devoured it. When *The Marshall Mathers LP* hit the stores in late May of 2000, it sold more than 1.8 million copies during the first week. The album set a record for single-week sales by a solo artist. By June 15, 2000, it had sold more than three million copies. If Em had not solidified himself as a bonafide rap master with his multi-platinum *The Slim Shady LP*, he would with *The Marshall Mathers LP*.

His latter album combined lyrics that were raunchy, gruesome, violent and offensive, but outrageously seductive and clever at the same time. Praised poured in. Dr. Dre, who had immediately recognized Eminem's superb talent, could not have been more pleased with his protégé.

"The success that Eminem has had is crazy," Dre remarked, "But it's deserved. Em is an incredible artist. He's a workaholic. He's wild and crazy, but he's serious when he gets behind that microphone."

Snoop Dogg called Em a genius. Jimmy Iovine proclaimed that "once in a great while, someone has a lightning rod right to the youth culture," and that Eminem was that guy. Iovine praised Eminen's story-telling ability, his wit and his imagination. Because Eminem was so clued in to youth culture, he could write movies or anything else, Iovine said. *The San Francisco Chronicle* agreed.

A *Chronicle* journalists wrote, "What makes Eminem a great rapper? He's a storyteller. "Kim," the prequel to his debut album's depiction of the imaginary murder of his ex-wife, is harrowing like a good Stephen King story. And "Stan," the tale of a psychotic fan who writes to his idol Eminem (complete with scratching pencil sounds), is a hip-hop *'Misery.'*"

As praise poured in, the CD was met with even more criticism than the prior LP. Rap detractors picked up where they left off on the *The Slim Shady LP* and railed against the misogynistic lyrics. But this time, they also blasted Eminem for comments that some people found to be anti-gay, although the rapper said that is not how he intended his rhymes to come across.

Eminem told Kurt Loder of *MTV* that his use of the word "faggot" on his album stemmed from his training as a battle emcee where the "lowest degrading thing that you can say to a man when you're battling him is call him a faggot and try to take away his manhood. Call him a sissy, call him a punk," he said, "Just like you might sit around in your living room and say, 'Dude, stop, you're being a fag, dude.' This does not necessarily mean you're being a gay person. It just means you're being a fag. That's the way that the word was always taught to me. That's how I learned the word. Battling with somebody, you do anything you can to strip their manhood away. I started getting people going, 'You have something against gay people,' and I thought it was funny. Because I don't."

The album was laced with profanity and came across as more hostile than his previous album. On the track "Kill You," Eminem says "Okay, I'm ready to go play. I've got the machete from O.J." And while killing is standard fodder for the genre,

Eminem pioneers new ground when he fantasizes about raping and killing his mother. Eminem ridicules his critics and enemies. In a pornographic skit, he makes fun of the Insane Clown Posse, who has joked on national television about having sex with his wife. He scoffs at American hypocrisy in "Who Knew." Hey says there must be some kind of mix-up that someone would ask him to fix up his lyrics as the president engages in scandalous extramarital liaisons. He lets you know he's not writing his music to please authority. On "The Real Slim Shady," he asks, "You think I give a damn about a Grammy?" Hmmm, put that way, one would guess not. Eminem caused the hair to stand on the necks of some parents just by remembering the Columbine High School murders/suicides. In one ditty, he says, "Don't blame me if little Eric jumps off the terrace, you should have been watching him. Apparently, you ain't parents."

While many of Eminem's fans laugh when he disses pop stars including 'N Sync, Will

Smith and Christina Aguilera, he took some heat about that as well. Em lashed back. He explained in an interview that he dissed Aguilera only in a response to disrespect she showed him first.

Eminem told CDNow, "She was on MTV running her mouth; she had her special, *What a Girl Wants*, and she was picking her top 10 videos or whatever. And she picked 'My Name Is,' and I was like, 'That's cool.' Then, as soon as the video went off, she just started demolishing me. I got married last year, like June or July, and nobody knew about that; it was something I didn't care for people to know as of yet. They already knew every thing else about me; it was like, can I keep one thing to myself? So she gets on there and says that she heard I was married; she didn't know for sure, she just heard it. And then she went on to say, 'Doesn't he have a song about killing his daughter's mother?' and started bashing me about domestic violence. So I'm like, why did (she) even pick my video if she was gonna pick it apart? She drew first blood, man, not me. She heard that I was married and didn't know for sure, so she went on national TV with it. I heard she did things with Fred Durst, and I heard she did things with Carson Daly, so I went on national TV with it. It's an eye for an eye."

Aguilera publicly denied the rumors. She said Eminem's comments about her and television personalities were absolutely untrue.

As for his dissing actor-rapper Will Smith, Eminem said, "I used to respect Will Smith (now) he's dissed the whole genre of rap. He dissed gangsta rap music. And that is one of the most influential musics out there. I respect him for saying his opinion, but not everybody is as happy as Will Smith. Not everybody sees life as happy and as posi- tive as he sees it. So if he wants to rap about birds and bees and flowers, then let him rap about birds and bees and flowers, but don't dis nobody else, dude. 'Nobody should cuss. If I don't cuss, nobody should cuss.' I felt like he was taking a stab at me and Dre and anybody who uses profanity on the records to express themselves. If you feel strong enough about something, then you might put a little 'fuck' before you say exactly what you're saying. 'This fucking tree,' if you feel that. It just depends on how you feel about something."

Eminem dismisses any notion that his music is harmful for his fans. On the contrary, he sees his music as a positive force.

"I'm not alone in feeling the way I feel," Eminem said on vh1.com. "I believe that a lot of people can relate to my shit—whether white, black, it doesn't matter. Everybody has been through some shit, whether it's drastic or not so drastic. Everybody gets to the point of 'I Don't Give a Fuck.'"

"I don't think music can make you kill or rape someone any more than a movie is going to make you do something you know is wrong," he said, maintaining that instead, it can give a person strength. "It can make a 15-year-old kid, who is being picked on by everyone and made to feel worthless, throw his middle finger up and say, 'Fuck you. You don't know who I am.' It can help make them respect their individuality, which is what music did for me. If people take anything from my music, it should be motivation to know that anything is possible as long as you keep working at it and don't back down. I didn' have nothin' going for me at school or at home until I found something I loved, which was music, and that changed everything."

Some fans even realized the artist's sensitive side, if it is okay for a rapper to have one. On the popular track "Stan," he raps advice to an obsessed fan: "I really think you and your girlfriend need each other. But maybe you just need to treat her better." But as he wrote advice to Stan, his own relationship was deteriorating while he recognized monumental career success. Em joked a lot about his wife in his music, but if the couple was having any significant problems, the public didn't see any real signs of it until around *The Marshall Mathers LP* debut. Shortly after the release of his second major album, Eminem was hanging out at a nightclub in suburban Detroit when an altercation took place between him and Douglas Dale, a man who worked for the Insane Clown Posse. Eminem allegedly pulled out a gun and threatened Dale. For that incident, he was charged with possession of a concealed weapon and for brandishing a firearm in public. Early the next morning, police charged Eminem with assault for striking another man who allegedly kissed his wife. Although he had managed to stay out of legal trouble for most of his life, the Michigan courtrooms would become a lot more familiar to Eminem.

He was scheduled for the major Up in Smoke Concert Tour with Dr. Dre and other rap heavyweights and a judge allowed him to keep that commitment. But soon after the tour took off, he faced devastating news about Kim. She had attended his concert at the Palace of Auburn Hills in Michigan, but after the concert she went home to Sterling Heights where she made an apparent suicide attempt. A spokesperson at Interscope confirmed Kim slashed her wrists. Emergency and fire department people were called to the scene where they treated her. She was rushed to the hospital and was further treated by doctors before being released the next day. Eminem was not at home when Kim slashed her wrists but expressed through a spokesperson that he was obviously concerned about his wife's well-being. He said they would handle things as privately as possible. Within weeks it was announced that Eminem had filed for a divorce.

Interscope replied, "The two have had an on-again, off-again relationship that's been extensively detailed in the press. In early June, the couple separated, and since then Eminem has come to the decision that a divorce is unavoidable."

Kim soon filed a suit seeking $10 million for intentional infliction of emotional distress as a result, in part, to Eminem's single "Kim," where he raps about killing his wife. The rapper's manager argued that his client is protected by "artistic expression" when he performs his music. Kim also sought sole custody of Hailie. Paul Rosenberg, went to bat for Eminem.

"Em's not going to be happy with that (Kim's lawsuit). Everybody on our side wanted to keep things low key and work things out amicably," Rosenberg told the *Detroit Free Press.*

Whatever Eminem's true feelings were, he managed to keep up a professional front. He kept on touring with the hugely successful "Up in Smoke" concert, accepted awards and promoted his album. Within weeks of Kim's suit, the couple settled out of court and Eminem was granted liberal privileges to visit his daughter.

Part III

The Dreem Team:
Dre + Em Uniting Rap Fans

You Forgot About Dre!

Chapter 9

Dr. Dre + Eminem
Take the Show On the Road

Dr. Dre and Eminem were riding high over the past two years with hit albums re-establishing and establishing their credibility. If they had left their command performances alone, they still would've been among music's crème de la crème. But they didn't. A piece was missing from the puzzle. Dre was determined to put together a concert tour that would be the mother of tours. He was in for a challenge. First, hip-hop concerts have long had a rap of falling short in the way of entertainment. Second, the shows were known for disruptions and violence. Dre was confident he could pull off a highly entertaining, smoothly run show. N.W.A. was negotiating a comeback with Snoop Dogg filling in for Eazy-E. The concert would be an opportunity to showcase the new N.W.A.

With the idea for his "Up in Smoke" tour gelling, Dre talked to Em and Snoop about joining the tour. They agreed and before it was over, he had an all-star line up that included Ice Cube, Warren G, Kurupt, MC Ren, Xzibit, Tha Eastsidaz, Mack 10, Nate Dogg and the Westside Connection. All the rappers turned out superb performances and shows sold out from coast to cost.

Glowing reviews were turning up in newspapers all over the country. In one review, the *San Francisco Chronicle* wrote "Deal with it: Rap rules. It rules the music charts, it rules fashion, it rules youth culture. Everyone from high school kids to *haute couture* designers to kiddie-pop bands wears it, sings it and emulates it. And on

Monday night, it ruled the sold-out San Jose Arena."

"The Up in Smoke tour…is probably the most star-studded hip-hop road show ever assembled. At its best, the show captured the kinetic beats and spontaneous word-play that inspired hip-hop at its inception some two decades ago."

The show was on from the moment the performers stepped onto the stage. It was colorful and energetic, from the perform-ers themselves, to the creativity in the stage designs. Fans got at least what they paid for. They cheered nonstop after Dre and Snoop Dogg's hour-long set that went down memory lane and through some of their best years as a recording and producing team. The stage set was designed like the back alley of a liquor store. A huge, talking skull loomed over it. The audience could not get enough of the rappers as they per-formed their hits including "Nuthin' But a G' Thang' and a rendition of "Let Me Ride," for which Snoop and Dre rolled onto stage in a ghetto-fabulous cruiser. "Still D.R.E." was a hit and "California Love" was dedicated to rap's dead artists: Eazy-E, the Notorious B.I.G., Big Punisher and Tupac Shakur. Snoop performed his own dynamic material and teamed up with Xzibit for the crowd-pleasing "B Please."

When Eminem took the stage, he was at his best for his 30-minute set. He performed his hot singles "The Real Slim Shady" and "Criminal," replicating the songs in their album quality. In his more outrageous moments, he dragged out a blow-up doll named Kim, roughed it up and tossed it to the audience.

"Yo, Cali, lemme ask you a question," he yelled to the audience. "How many of you ever get angry? How many get so pissed off they could fucking kill somebody?" When the crowd responded letting him know it felt his vibe, Em yelled, "all right, next time go home and play this song instead."

After Em's set, he reappeared to team up with Dre on the songs "Forgot About Dre" and "What's the Difference." When it was Ice Cube's turn, he was lowered to the stage in a chamber with snow swirling above it. He quickly thawed out and led Mack 10 and the Westside Connection through vintage Cube's "Bow Down," "Check Yo Self," and "It Was a Good Day." From his latest album *War and Peace: The Peace Disc*, he performed "Hello" with MC Ren.

The night at the San Jose stadium ended with a glimpse at the possible N.W.A. reunion with Snoop, Dre, Ice Cube and MC Ren performing a brief encore rendition of the new song "Chin Check." The successful show in San Jose was similar to other shows across the country. And not to be overlooked was the fact that Eminem had attracted a large following of new fans.

Chapter 10

The Next Episode

As for the future of his music, Dre says he plans to keep being original and staying away from sampling. "I don't think it's possible for hip-hop to grow if producers just keep copying what has already been done," he said. "I used those old records simply as my motivation but I try to stay away from sampling. There are times I might use it, but I'm not going to base a whole album around someone else's music."

Dre took part in the directing of the "Forgot About Dre," video, featuring Eminem, and he's planning to do more directing. He laughs and says modestly that he might try his hand at movie direction. But it's a good possibility that that lies in the near future. He has written a movie script called "Please Listen to My Demo," which is his life story.

And *Aftermath* promises to get even bigger and better. Dre intends to keep on making music because it is simply what he has been called to do. "I can't really explain it because for me, it's like breathing," he says. "I believe I was put on this planet to make hip-hop music. There are times when I get tired of being in the studio, but that only lasts about two weeks, then I got to go do my thing. Hey, I would do this shit for nothing…that's how strong my passion is."

Dre predicts Hittman will be the label's next superstar: "Hittman is our next protege. He's the next person that we're going to groom and try to build into a superstar, super hip-hop star. He's incredible. He could sing, his rhymes are ridiculous, and his delivery is incredible. That's why he's heard on the album probably more than I am, you know what I'm sayin'. He's incredible. And he's a real cool, laid-back guy, you know, so I know outside of the studio he's not going to do anything to ruin his career."

As for Eminem, he has pending legal issues to overcome but he will undoubt-edly come through in fine form in the end. He is being courted by Hollywood and may appear with Denzel Washington in a dramatic film. He is starting his own record label. At this point in his career, there is no question the rapper's talent and popularity are his ticket to most anywhere he chooses to travel.

Dr. Dre Discography
Dr. Dre 2001

1999

1. Lolo (Intro)
2. The Watcher
3. You
4. Still D.R.E.
5. Big Ego's
6. Xxplosive
7. What's The Difference
8. Bar One
9. Light Speed
10. Forgot About Dre
11. The Next Episode
12. Let's Get High
13. Bitch Niggaz
14. The Car Bomb
15. Murder Ink
16. Ed-Ucation
17. Some L.A. Niggaz
18. Pause 4 Porno
19. Housewife
20. Ackrite
21. Bang Bang
22. The Message

Performers: Dr. Dre, Mary J. Blige, Defari, Nate Dogg, Eminem, Eddie Griffin, Hittman, K, King T, Kokane, Kurupt, MC Ren, Mel-Man, Traci Nelson, Rell, Snoop Doggy Dogg, Time Bomb and Xzibit.

Dr. Dre Presents...The Aftermath
1996

1. Aftermath - (The Intro)
2. East Coast / West Coast Killas
3. Sh**tin On The World
4. Blunt Time
5. Been There Done That
6. Choices
7. As The Worl Keeps Turning
8. Got Me Open
9. Str-8 Gone
10. Please
11. Do 4 Love
12. Sexy Dance
13. No Second Chance
14. L.A.W. (Lyrical Assault Weapon)
15. Nationowl
16. Fame

Performers: Dr. Dre, Ruben Cruz, D-Ruff, Flossy P, Hands-On, Group Therapy, Nicole Johnson, Mel-Man, King T, Jheryl Lockhart, Mike Lynn, Cassandra McCowan, Sid McCoy, RBX, RC, Stu-B-Doo, Kim Summerson, Whoz Who and Maurice Wilcher.

The Chronic

1992

1. The Cronic (Intro)
2. Wit Dre Day (And Everybody's Celebratin')
3. Let Me Ride
4. The Day The Niggaz Took Over
5. Nothin' But A 'G' Thang
6. Deeez Nuuuts
7. Lil' Ghetto Boy
8. A Nigga Witta Gun
9. Rat-Tat-Tat-Tat
10. The $20 Sack Pyramid
11. Lyrical Gangbang
12. High Powered
13. The Doctor's Office
14. Stranded Of Death Row
15. The Roach (The Chronic Outro)

Performers: Dr. Dre, RBX, Daz, Snoop, D.O.C. and Kurupt.

Dr. Dre's N.W.A. Recordings

N.W.A. Legacy 1988-98
N.W.A. Anniversary Tribute 1998
Greatest Hits 1996
Niggaz4life 1991
Straight Outta Compton 1988
N.W.A. & The Posse 1987

Also,

Producer for major recording artists including Snoop Dogg, Tupac Shakur and Eminem.

He has contributed to the following movie soundtracks:

> *Bullworth, Natural Born Killers, Deep Cover, Wild Wild West* and *Friday.*

Eminem Discography

Marshall Mathers LP

2000

1. Public Service Announcement 2000
2. Kill You
3. Stan
4. Paul (Skit)
5. Who Knew
6. Steve Berman
7. The Way I Am
8. The Real Slim Shady
9. Remember Me?
10. I'm Back
11. Marshall Mathers
12. Ken Kaniff (Skit)
13. Drug Ballad
14. Amityville
15. B***** Please II
16. Kim
17. Under The Influence
18. Criminal

Performer: Eminem

The Slim Shady LP

1999

1. Public Service Announcement
2. My Name Is
3. Guilty Conscience
4. Brain Damage
5. Paul
6. If I Had Bass
7. 97' Bonnie & Clyde Bass
8. Bitch
9. Role Model
10. Lounge
11. My Fault
12. Ken Kaniff
13. Cum On Everybody
14. Rock Bottom
15. Just Don't Give A Fuck
16. Soap
17. As The World Turns
18. I'm Shady
19. Bad Meets Evil
20. Still Don't Give A Fuck

Performers: Eminem, Dr. Dre, Jeff Bass and Marky Bass and Royce Da 5.

Also,

Infinite 1996

He has contributed to the following Soundtracks:

Next Friday and *End of Days*.

Kid Rock performed his song, "Devil Without a Cause."

Kelly Kenyatta is a Chicago-based journalist who has written for many national publications including the *Chicago Tribune, Black Enterprise Magazine, The Los Angeles Times* and the *Indianapolis Star-News.* She is also the author of *Yes, Yes, Yes: The Unauthorized Biography of Destiny's Child.*

ORDER FORM

BUSTA BOOKS

Fax Orders: 480-283-0991   Telephone Orders: 480-460-1660
Postal Orders: Send Checks & Money Orders to: Busta Books
Online Orders: E-mail: bustabks@aol.com
1334 E. Chandler Blvd., Suite 5-D67, Phoenix, AZ 85048

Please send:
_____ copy/ies of *You Forgot About Dre: The Unauthorized Biography of Dr. Dre & Eminem*

_____ copy/ies of *Yes, Yes, Yes: The Unauthorized Biography of Destiny's Child*

Name:_____

Company Name:_____

Address:_____

_____

City:_____State:_____Zip:_____

Telephone: (_____) _____

E-mail:_____

For Bulk Rates Call: **480-460-1660**

Yes, Yes, Yes:The Unauthorized Biography of Destiny's Child $4.95
You Forgot About Dre: The Unauthorized Biography of
Dr. Dre & Eminem $10.95

❏ Check ❏ Money Order ❏ Cashiers Check
❏ Credit Card:
   ❏ MC ❏ Visa ❏ Amex ❏ Discover

CC#_____   Expiration
Date:_____

Payable to: **Shipping:** $3.00 for first book
   Busta Books $1.00 each additional book.
   1334 E. Chandler Blvd., Suite 5-D67   Allow 7 days for delivery.
   Phoenix, AZ 85048   **Sales Tax:** Add 7.05% to books
                                             shipped to AZ addresses.

Total enclosed: $_____

ORDER FORM

BUSTA BOOKS

Fax Orders: 480-283-0991   Telephone Orders: 480-460-1660
Postal Orders: Send Checks & Money Orders to: Busta Books
Online Orders: E-mail: bustabks@aol.com
1334 E. Chandler Blvd., Suite 5-D67, Phoenix, AZ 85048

Please send:
_____ copy/ies of *You Forgot About Dre: The Unauthorized Biography of Dr. Dre & Eminem*

_____ copy/ies of *Yes, Yes, Yes: The Unauthorized Biography of Destiny's Child*

Name:_____

Company Name:_____

Address:_____

_____

City:_____State:_____Zip:_____

Telephone: (_____) _____

E-mail:_____

For Bulk Rates Call: **480-460-1660**

Yes, Yes, Yes:The Unauthorized Biography of Destiny's Child	$4.95
You Forgot About Dre: The Unauthorized Biography of	
Dr. Dre & Eminem	$10.95

❏ Check ❏ Money Order ❏ Cashiers Check
❏ Credit Card:
   ❏ MC ❏ Visa ❏ Amex ❏ Discover

CC#_____   Expiration
Date:_____

Payable to: **Shipping:** $3.00 for first book
  Busta Books $1.00 each additional book.
  1334 E. Chandler Blvd., Suite 5-D67   Allow 7 days for delivery.
  Phoenix, AZ 85048   **Sales Tax:** Add 7.05% to books
                                          shipped to AZ addresses.

Total enclosed: $_____